NATIONAL GEOGRAPHIC

T0040065

Flowers for Grandma

Karl Jensen

CLOUCE

red

orange

yellow

purple

white

pink

blue

green

To
Grandma

red

orange

yellow

purple

white

pink

blue

green